Amazing Nature

Magnificent Movers

Tim Knight

Heinemann
LIBRARY

www.heinemann.co.uk/library

Visit our website to find out more information about **Heinemann Library** books.

To order:

☎ Phone 44 (0) 1865 888066

▤ Send a fax to 44 (0) 1865 314091

▢ Visit the Heinemann Bookshop at www.heinemann.co.uk/library to browse our catalogue and order online.

First published in Great Britain by Heinemann Library, Halley Court, Jordan Hill, Oxford OX2 8EJ, part of Harcourt Education. Heinemann is a registered trademark of Harcourt Education Ltd.

© Harcourt Education Ltd 2003
The moral right of the proprietor has been asserted.

Editorial: Jilly Attwood and Claire Throp
Design: David Poole and Geoff Ward
Picture Research: Peter Morris
Production: Séverine Ribierre

Originated by Ambassador Litho Ltd
Printed in China by South China Printing Company

ISBN 0 431 16660 9
07 06 05 04 03
10 9 8 7 6 5 4 3 2 1

British Library Cataloguing in Publication Data
Knight, Tim
Magnificent Movers - (Amazing Nature)
591.4'79
A full catalogue record for this book is available from the British Library.

Acknowledgements
The publishers would like to thank the following for permission to reproduce photographs:
Ardea pp. **6** (Pascal Goetgheluck), **10** (Jean Paul Ferrero), **12** (left) (K. & L. Laidler), **19** (Hayden Oake), **20** (Francois Gohier); Bruce Coleman pp. **4** (Gerald S. Cubitt), **11** (Sarah Cook), **12** (right), **13** (Jorg and Petra Wegner), **14** (right) (Mary Plage), **24** (Staffan Widstrand), **25** (Wayne Lankinen); Corbis pp. **16** (Michael & Patricia Fogden), **23** (Chase Swift); FLPA pp. **7** (Silvestris), **21**, **22** (Minden Pictures); NHPA pp. **5** (ANT), **8**, **9** (Martin Harvey), **15** (E. A. Janes), **17** (Nigel J. Dennis), **18**, **26**, **27** (Stephen Dalton); Tim Knight p. **14** (left)

Cover photograph of a flying squirrel reproduced with permission of Oxford Scientific Films/Photo Researchers.

X

Contents

Any words appearing in the text in bold, **like this**, are explained in the Glossary.

On the move

Animals spend most of their lives on the move. They have to find food and a mate, catch their **prey** and escape their enemies. Sometimes they must travel long distances. To do these things, some have become experts at running, jumping, crawling or flying. Others can walk upside down, swim backwards or climb trees.

Animals that move in a particularly strange way are often given names to describe how they get around. Be prepared to meet sidewinders and roadrunners, spring hares and pond skaters.

Tree kangaroos are expert climbers. Instead of hopping on the ground, they leap from branch to branch, using their long tails to help them balance.

Plant movement

Plants must move too. Although most are rooted to the spot, they have moving parts. As they grow, they reach out to fill new spaces or find ways of climbing towards the sunlight. Many plants use wind power, producing seeds that may be blown long distances on the breeze. Seeds may also be transported by water and even by animals, getting caught in fur or spread in their droppings.

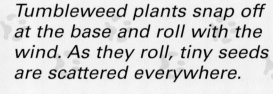

Tumbleweed plants snap off at the base and roll with the wind. As they roll, tiny seeds are scattered everywhere.

Slow motion

Most plants move too slowly for the human eye to see, but we can watch them in action if we speed up their movements using **time-lapse photography**. When an old tree falls, it creates a gap in the forest **canopy**. Life-giving sunlight reaches the forest floor, giving the young plants the energy that they need to grow taller. The fastest growing plants, called **pioneers**, are the first to fill the gap. They race upwards towards the sunlight. Other plants move more slowly and may take years to grow just a few centimetres, but one day they may overtake their faster-growing neighbours, which soon reach their full height.

Bamboo is one of the world's fastest growing plants.

A sloth's slow-motion movements make it more difficult for **predators** to spot.

Slowcoaches

Moving slowly can be an advantage in the animal kingdom too. Sharp movements can attract the attention of an eagle-eyed hunter. In the tree-tops of South America, the sloth hangs upside down from a branch. It clings on with its hooked claws and slender limbs. Lifting one leg at a time, it moves like a hairy robot whose batteries are almost flat.

The slow loris lives in the rainforests of south-east Asia. At night it moves slowly through branches to feed on fruit, while most of its enemies are asleep. Africa's slow-motion climber, the potto, also feeds after dark. Its hands and feet are like those of a monkey, helping it to grip the branches as it searches for a meal.

High speed

In the shelter of the forest, it may pay to move slowly. For creatures that live out in the open, speed is more important.

The sailfish is an underwater sprinter, reaching speeds up to 110 kilometres per hour. Its pointed head and **streamlined** body help it to move smoothly through the water. The sailfish is the fastest fish in the sea.

Two-legged race

The ostrich cannot fly, but it can outrun most **predators**. Its long, powerful legs carry it at speeds up to 70 kilometres per hour. In just two strides, an ostrich can travel further than the Olympic long jump record. The roadrunner prefers not to fly, even though it can. Instead, this bird runs hotfoot across the desert, chasing insects and **reptiles**.

The tsessebe is one of the fastest kinds of antelope in Africa, and uses its speed to escape predators.

Long legs and **shock-absorbent** hooves help Africa's **grazing** animals, such as gazelles, to make a quick getaway. One of their most dangerous enemies is the cheetah, the fastest animal on land. The cheetah is a lightweight, long-legged cat, with a flexible spine and a long, thin body. It is built for short bursts of speed, and hunts by outsprinting gazelles and other antelope.

Spring time

Running can be hard work, especially over a long distance. Hopping and jumping allows animals to move around quickly, find food or escape danger, without wasting too much energy.

Australia's kangaroos and wallabies are probably the best-known hoppers, but there are others. The African spring hare and the jerboa, a long-tailed desert mouse, behave like miniature kangaroos. They hop away quickly at the first sign of trouble.

The caracal is a large African cat, with unusually long and very powerful hind legs. It uses them to catch its **prey** by springing high into a tree or launching itself through the air.

At the highest point of its hop, a kangaroo may be 3 metres above the ground.

Bouncing bushbabies

In the African night, bushbabies bounce around among the tree branches like furry rubber balls. Their powerful legs help them to leap over 2 metres into the air from a crouching position. This carries them quickly out of the reach of **predators**. They steer with their long tails while they are in mid-air, and use their tails to balance as they land.

Jumping spiders also hunt with the help of springy legs, but their power does not come from extra large muscles. Instead, they tense their muscles with lightning quick speed. This forces body fluid into their legs, causing them to straighten and catapult the spider into the air.

The sifaka, a kind of lemur, cannot run on all fours because its arms are much shorter than its extra-long legs. It hops around instead, holding its arms out to balance.

Swingers

Jumping and leaping is a useful way to travel, but for creatures that live high above the ground it can also be dangerous. A fall from the tree-tops would cause serious injury. Animals that spend most of their lives in the trees need to be experts at moving through the branches.

Most monkeys and apes are excellent climbers, with good balance. Eyes on the front of their head, rather than on each side, help them to judge distance. They have grasping hands and feet to hold on to the branches.

A spider monkey can hang by its tail, leaving its hands free to reach for fruit or leaves.

Tail links

Monkeys are not the only animals to use their tails for climbing. Two tree-climbing anteaters, the South American tamandua and the long-tailed pangolin from Africa, both have **prehensile** tails.

When climbing down a tree, the long-tailed pangolin wraps its tail around the trunk or a branch to give it extra grip.

King of the swingers

A male orang-utan is the heaviest tree-living animal in the world, weighing up to 100 kilograms. Instead of balancing on branches, he hangs underneath them and swings from tree to tree. This way of moving is known as **brachiating**.

The gibbon, a lightweight cousin of the orang-utan, is probably the most amazing acrobat in the forest. Gibbons swing through the tree-tops at high speed. They throw themselves across wide gaps, using their hands like hooks to grab the branches in their path. The gibbon is truly the king of the swingers.

Orang-utans use their feet as an extra pair of hands. Their hips are 'double-jointed', which means that their legs can reach out at weird angles.

Climbers

While some creatures spend their whole life in the tree-tops, others are just visitors searching for food or shelter. Unless they can fly, these visitors need to be good climbers.

Some animals can walk up smooth or slippery surfaces. Tree frogs have sticky pads on the tips of their toes, which act as suckers and help them to climb. A climbing cockroach produces small amounts of fluid from its feet, which works like a non-setting glue.

A gecko's foot is covered in about half a million microscopic hairs. At the tip of each hair are thousands of tiny pads. Ten million of these pads would fit on a pinhead. When the gecko slides its foot forward, the tiny hairs grip the surface underneath like extra-strong velcro. To lift its foot again, the gecko slides it in the opposite direction.

Geckos can climb up a pane of glass, or even walk upside down across a ceiling.

Bears climb by hugging the trunk and 'shinning up' the tree in lightning quick time. Their powerful claws help them to grip the bark. Leopards and jaguars are the best climbers among the big cats. They leap as high as they can, then use claw and muscle power to pull themselves further up.

Plant climbers

Some plants are expert climbers too. The long, thin stem of a rattan palm is lined with needle-sharp, backward-facing **barbs**. It grows upwards towards the light and hooks onto anything in its path. Ivy sprouts thin roots all along its climbing stems, which cling to any rough surface. Tropical glory lilies use their long, curling leaf tips as hooks, latching on to the nearest support.

Bindweed climbs by winding itself around the stem of other plants, including farmers' crops.

Crawlers

Animals without arms or legs have to rely on other parts of their body to help them move around.

The horned rattlesnake is found in the deserts of Mexico and south-west USA. This snake has found a clever way to cross loose, shifting sand. It moves by rolling its body sideways in a series of graceful 'S' shaped loops and is nicknamed the 'sidewinder'.

The horned rattlesnake is not the only snake known as a sidewinder. In Africa's Namib Desert two kinds of adder, the Namaqua dwarf adder and Peringuey's adder, also move sideways across the sand and have the same nickname.

At any time, only two points of a sidewinder's body are touching the hot sand. The snake leaves behind a pattern in the sand that looks like a series of parallel loops.

Slow and slimy

Snails and slugs move with the help of muscles in their foot. Tensing these muscles causes a rippling movement along the sole of the foot. This movement runs like a wave from back to front, and pulls the snail forward. The foot also produces a sticky slime, called mucus. This helps snails to glide smoothly across rough or sharp objects without hurting themselves. It also helps them to crawl uphill.

Some fish move around on land, using their fins as 'legs'. The climbing perch sometimes crosses dry land in search of cleaner water. It moves across country by wriggling its tail, while the front of its body is propped up by its stiff **pectoral** fins and spiny gill covers.

Mudskippers leave the water to feed on insects. They skip forward with a flick of their tail, or drag themselves across the mud using their front fins like a pair of crutches.

Walking on water

Some animals, including ones that cannot swim, have found ways of moving across water without sinking.

Pond skaters skim across the water's surface. They spread their weight across long, thin, waterproof legs. Hairy, wax-coated feet allow them to stand on the water without breaking the **surface tension**. This is a kind of elastic skin formed by water droplets sticking together. Pond skaters dart around at over a metre per second and can also jump up to 50 centimetres into the air.

The basilisk lizard moves so quickly that its feet only touch the water's surface for a split second – not long enough to break the surface tension.

The jacana uses floating water lily leaves as stepping stones. Its enormous feet and long toes help to spread the bird's weight and stop it sinking.

Water-skiing beetle

The camphor beetle jet-skis across the water to escape **predators**. The beetle releases a special substance from its rear. This substance reduces the water surface tension behind it, so the beetle is pulled forward by the surface tension in front. It shoots forwards, holding out its front feet like skis. It steers by using the tip of its body as a **rudder**.

Moving underwater

Swimming is difficult, but most fish make it look easy. The fastest swimmers, such as sharks and tuna, have pointed heads and **streamlined** bodies. These features help them to move through the water at amazing speeds. A powerful tail fin drives them forward. Other fins help them to brake, balance or change direction quickly.

Most fish swim by bending their bodies in an S-shaped wave. The Amazon knife fish keeps its body straight. Instead of a tail fin and a **dorsal fin** on its back, it has one long fin running along its underside from head to tail. It can shoot forwards or reverse quickly with just a flick of this fin.

The dolphin's powerful tail, called a fluke, helps it to leap up to 7 metres out of the water.

Many **mammals**, birds and **reptiles** are excellent swimmers too. The otter paddles with its webbed toes, and uses its strong tail as a **rudder**. A swimming penguin steers with its feet. Sea turtles drive themselves forward with their front flippers, using them as paddles.

Jet power

An octopus can walk on its tentacles, but it uses 'jet propulsion' to avoid trouble. It sucks water into a special chamber through a kind of **funnel**. It uses powerful muscles to force the water out again at high speed and shoot itself forward.

The squid also uses jet power. It controls which way it travels by squirting out water through a pipe that can be pointed in different directions.

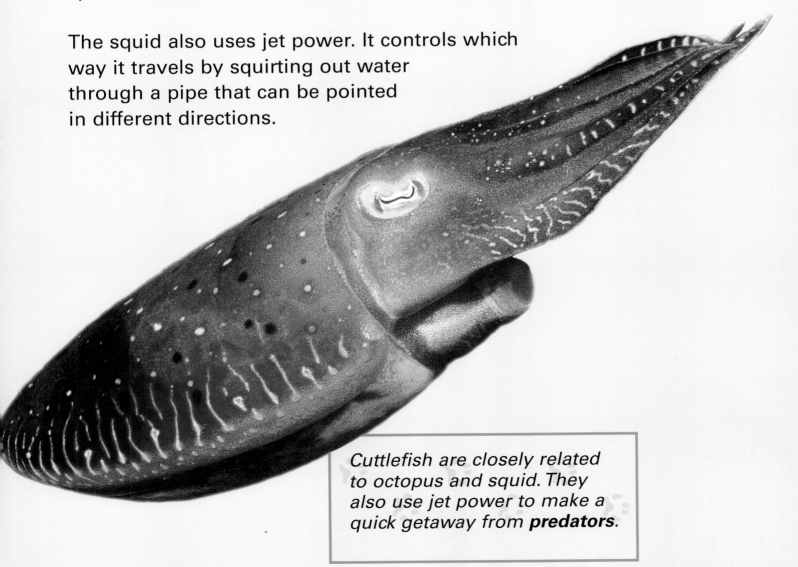

*Cuttlefish are closely related to octopus and squid. They also use jet power to make a quick getaway from **predators**.*

Wind and wing power

Moving through air is much easier than moving through water. Some animals and plants use wind power to help them move from place to place. Others have their own wings.

Blowing in the wind

A plant that uses wind power needs its seeds to travel as far away as possible. Otherwise they will be competing with their parent for water, light and food. Seeds produced by tall trees often have 'wings', which help them to glide long distances before reaching the ground. Some seeds have a pair of wings of different length, which means that they do not spin straight down to the ground. The seeds fall at an angle instead, and land well away from the parent tree.

The wings of a falling seed spin like helicopter blades, keeping it in the air long enough for the breeze to blow it sideways.

Even the fastest insects cannot dodge an agile predator such as this dazzling flycatcher.

Powered flight

Insect wings produce their own power. Bumblebees need broad wings and strong muscles to lift their bodies into the air. On cold mornings, they warm these muscles by 'shivering' their wings from side to side. The tiny hoverfly not only hovers, but also darts sideways and even flies backwards. It can change direction in 30 thousandths of a second and reach speeds above 40 kilometres an hour.

Flying lessons

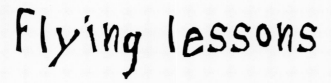

Birds are masters of the air. They swoop, soar, glide, hover, and perform spectacular aerobatics. Their feathers, which are **aerodynamic**, help them to fly smoothly through the air. Bird feathers are made of a strong, lightweight material called **keratin**. Hollow or paper-thin bones also help to reduce a bird's weight, so its wings have to work less hard to keep its body in the air.

Those birds that live in thick forest often have short, stubby wings. This makes it easier to swerve and dodge in a tight space. Flycatchers live up to their names, twisting and turning in mid-air to snap up a passing insect.

Vultures soar high in the sky. They ride on warm air **currents**, called **thermals**. These columns of hot air rise from the ground like steam from a kettle. The vulture's broad wings have a large surface area, which helps to catch the rising air.

The condor has a wingspan of 3.5 metres. It can glide without any effort, hour after hour.

Flying backwards

Hummingbirds hover in front of flowers while they sip **nectar**. They can even fly backwards. Their tiny wings move in a figure of eight. They beat their wings so quickly that they look more like buzzing insects than birds. As a hummingbird darts to and fro, like a miniature helicopter, its heart beats an incredible 1000 times a minute.

By drinking from a flower in mid-air, hummingbirds are able to feed on nectar that other birds cannot reach.

Gliders

Animals without wings have found ways to 'fly' too. Flying lizards need to travel from tree to tree in search of food. The forest floor can be a dangerous place, so they avoid crossing it by turning themselves into tiny hang-gliders.

When flying lizards launch themselves into the air from high in a tree, they fan out their ribs into a pair of stiff flaps. These flaps fold and unfold like a pair of **retractable** wings and help them to glide to the next tree.

The colugo, also called the flying lemur, is completely covered in a furry cloak that stretches from its neck to the tip of its tail. The rectangular shape of the cloak makes the colugo look like a flying doormat.

Male flying lizards sometimes chase each other in mid-air, dodging and weaving between the tree trunks.

The greater glider is as big as a cat. The tiny feathertail glider is the size of a small mouse. Both these Australian **marsupials** glide with the help of loose flaps of skin along their sides, using their long tail as a **rudder**.

The flying fish shoots out of the water to escape **predators**. It can glide above the surface for hundreds of metres, using a pair of stiff, extra-long fins as wings.

The most amazing glider of all is the flying snake. It flattens its body and 'swims' through the air. The snake can even change direction by squirming as it flies.

Wallace's flying frog uses its webbed feet as miniature parachutes to leap through the tree-tops.

Fact file

The fastest animal on land, a sprinting cheetah can reach over 100 kilometres per hour.

A spinner dolphin can twist its body up to seven times in a single leap.

A sifaka lemur can jump over 10 metres in one leap.

A spider monkey can eat with both hands while hanging only by its **prehensile** tail.

Jet-propelled squid can reach such high speeds that they sometimes shoot out of the water and land on the deck of a ship.

The world's biggest frog, the goliath frog from West Africa, can jump over 3 metres.

Before starting to hunt, the roadrunner basks in the sun like a lizard. Once it has warmed up, it can run at speeds of over 25 kilometres per hour.

The wandering albatross is built for high-speed gliding. It has a wingspan of 3.5 metres and can keep flying for weeks on end.

Jumping spiders can jump up to 50 times their own body length.

Scientists have worked out that the hairs on a gecko's foot have a strong enough grip to support the weight of a small child.

The hobby, a long-winged falcon, is fast and agile enough to catch dragonflies and swifts in mid-air.

Swifts fly continuously for nine months a year, feeding, sleeping and even mating on the wing.

The bee hummingbird is the smallest bird in the world. It beats its wings up to 200 times a second.

The world's smallest gliding **mammal** is the feathertail glider. It is named after the rows of stiff hairs on either side of its bald tail.

Wallace's flying frog can glide a distance of 80 metres.

A hovering kestrel stays in exactly the same position in mid-air. It does this by facing into the wind and flying forward at the same speed as the wind is blowing.

Birdwing butterflies have large, broad wings that are perfect for gliding through the tree-tops. Queen Alexandra's birdwing has a wingspan of almost 30 centimetres and is the largest butterfly in the world.

Glossary

aerodynamic shaped to allow smooth flight through the air

barb hook

brachiating using arms to swing from branch to branch through the trees

canopy tree-tops

current flowing water or air

dorsal fin fin on the back of a fish

funnel object with a wide opening that gradually narrows into a tube

graze eat grass

keratin strong, lightweight substance from which feathers and human nails are made

mammal animal that feeds its young on milk

marsupial animal that keeps its young in a pouch

nectar sugary liquid produced by flowers

pectoral growing on the chest

pioneer fast growing, usually short-lived plant that quickly fills a gap in the forest

predator animal that hunts and kills other living creatures

prehensile able to grasp like a hand

prey animal that is killed and eaten by predators

reptile scaly, cold-blooded animal such as a snake or a lizard

retractable able to be pulled or folded back into the body

rudder tool used for steering

shock-absorbent giving protection against hard bangs

streamlined smooth and pointed to improve movement through air or water

surface tension kind of elastic skin formed by water droplets sticking together

thermal rising current of warm air

time-lapse photography a way of filming very slow action by taking many single pictures over a long period of time, then putting them together and speeding them up to show the action happening very quickly

Index

Titles in the *Amazing Nature* series include:

Hardback   0 431 16652 8

Hardback   0 431 16650 1

Hardback   0 431 16651 X

Hardback   0 431 16662 5

Hardback   0 431 16660 9

Hardback   0 431 16653 6

Hardback   0 431 16661 7

Hardback   0 431 16663 3

Find out about the other titles in this series on our website www.heinemann.co.uk/library